A QUICK HISTORY OF THE MAYAN CIVILIZATION

History for Kids
Children's History Books

BABY PROFESSOR
EDUCATION KIDS

Speedy Publishing LLC

40 E. Main St. #1156

Newark, DE 19711

www.speedypublishing.com

Copyright 2017

The Mayans created one of the great civilizations of the Americas, before the arrival of the Europeans. Let's look at the story of the rise and fall of their empire.

Mayans

THE ARRIVAL OF THE MAYANS

The ancestors of the Mayans probably crossed to North America from Asia, walking across a land bridge that existed about twenty thousand years ago. All the hundreds of cultures and civilizations of the Americas are probably descended from those first arrivals.

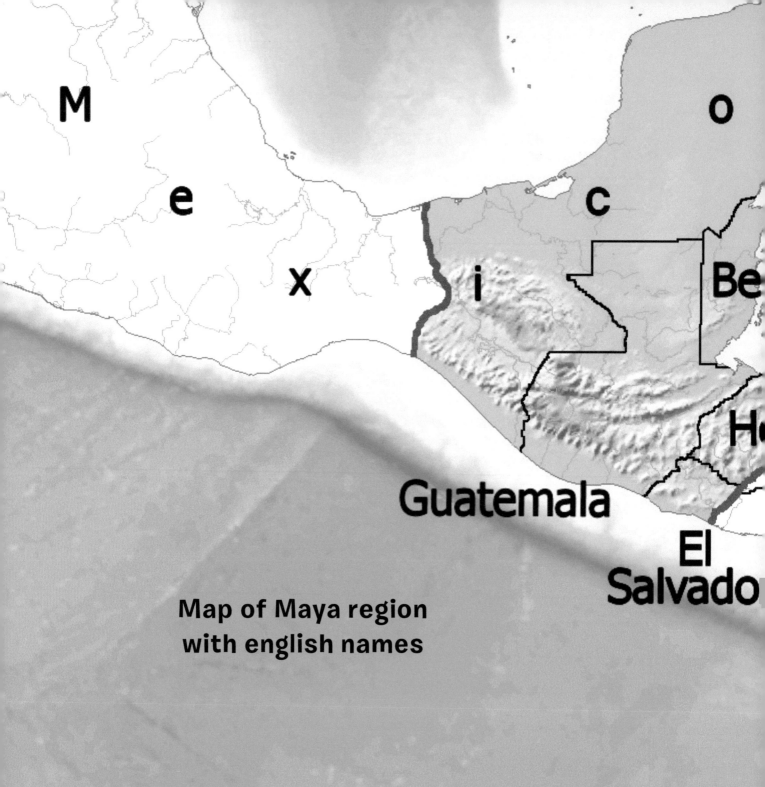

M
e
x
i
c
o
Be

He

Guatemala

El
Salvado

Map of Maya region
with english names

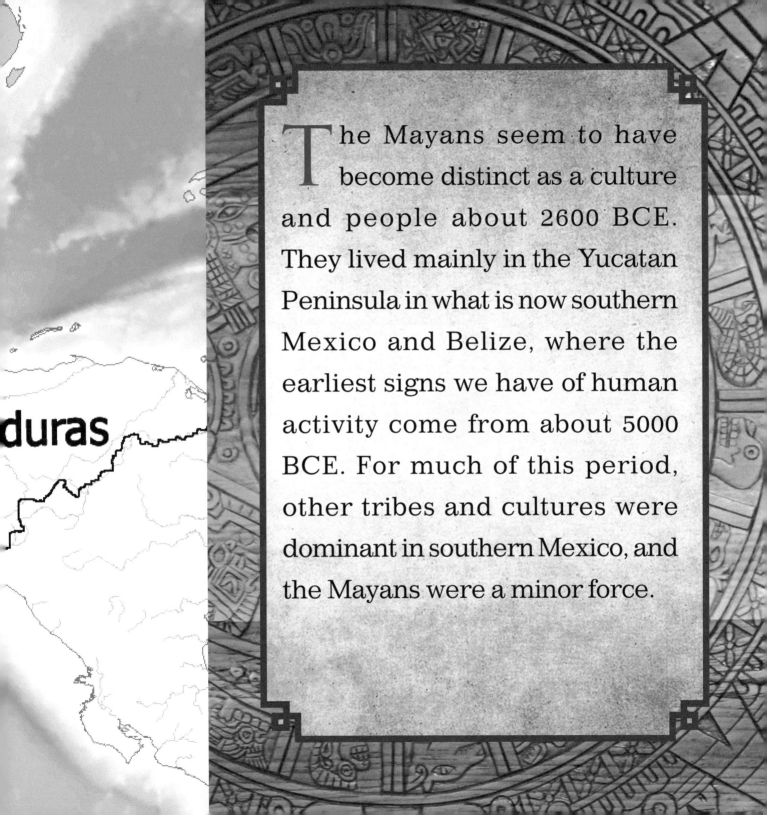

duras

The Mayans seem to have become distinct as a culture and people about 2600 BCE. They lived mainly in the Yucatan Peninsula in what is now southern Mexico and Belize, where the earliest signs we have of human activity come from about 5000 BCE. For much of this period, other tribes and cultures were dominant in southern Mexico, and the Mayans were a minor force.

Olmec Colossal Head

The Mayans drew on the ideas, customs, and inventions of earlier civilizations about which we know very little, like the Olmecs.

They became very wise in astronomy, and they developed complex calendars to track both the year and the cycles of important religious festivals. They developed a complex and subtle writing system.

Everything the Mayans built, from huge cities to underground reservoirs to store rain water in areas without rivers or lakes, was done without metal tools or animals like horses or oxen to help haul things.

THE RISE OF THE MAYANS

The Mayans, according to legends and the little archaeological evidence we have, arrived in the Yucatan from the west. Their rise to a controlling position in the area seems to have begun about 200 CE.

Mayan Zodiac Circle

Kukulcan, a priest and teacher, is understood to have been the founder of the Mayan Empire. Under him, the Mayans were divided into four kingdoms, ruled by four noble families. Kukulcan's kingdom ruled over the other three kingdoms, and his city, Mayapan, became the capital of the empire.

Mayapan

All the kings had to live for part of each year at Mayapan until the eleventh century.

Uxmal, Governor's Palace

Then there was a revolt of the lesser kings, and Mayapan was destroyed. The new capital was Uxmal, the city of a different tribe.

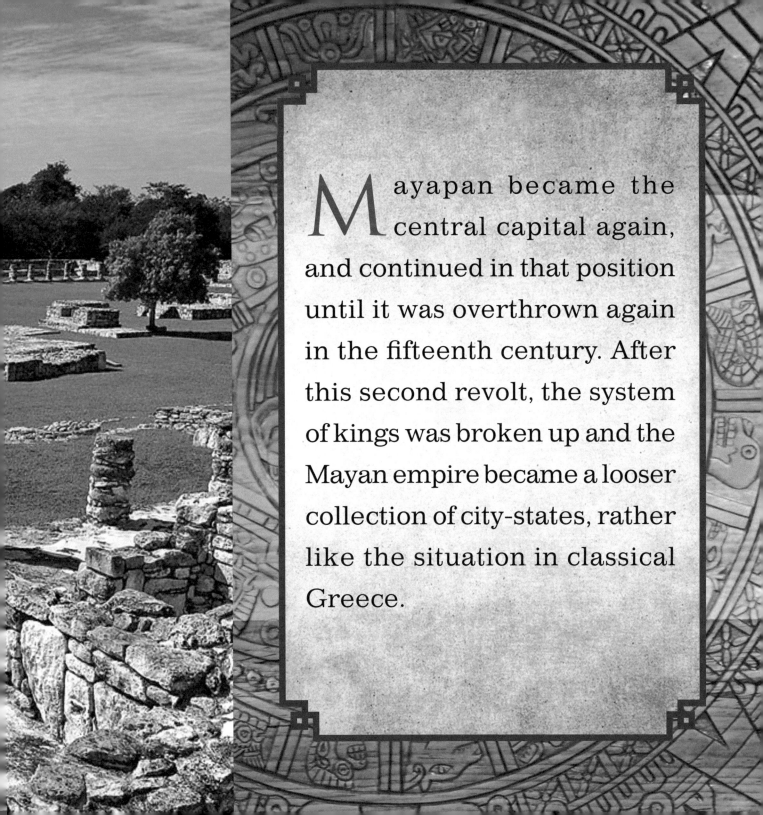

Mayapan became the central capital again, and continued in that position until it was overthrown again in the fifteenth century. After this second revolt, the system of kings was broken up and the Mayan empire became a looser collection of city-states, rather like the situation in classical Greece.

MAYAN CULTURE

The Mayan civilization was rich and complex. It was the only culture in the Americas that not only created a system of writing, but used that system to record and celebrate its history. The Mayans carved pillars and slabs of stone with stories about what their great kings and heroes had done, and set the carvings up in public places where anybody could read and learn the story. They also made records on pottery, paper, and cured skins.

Mayan Writing

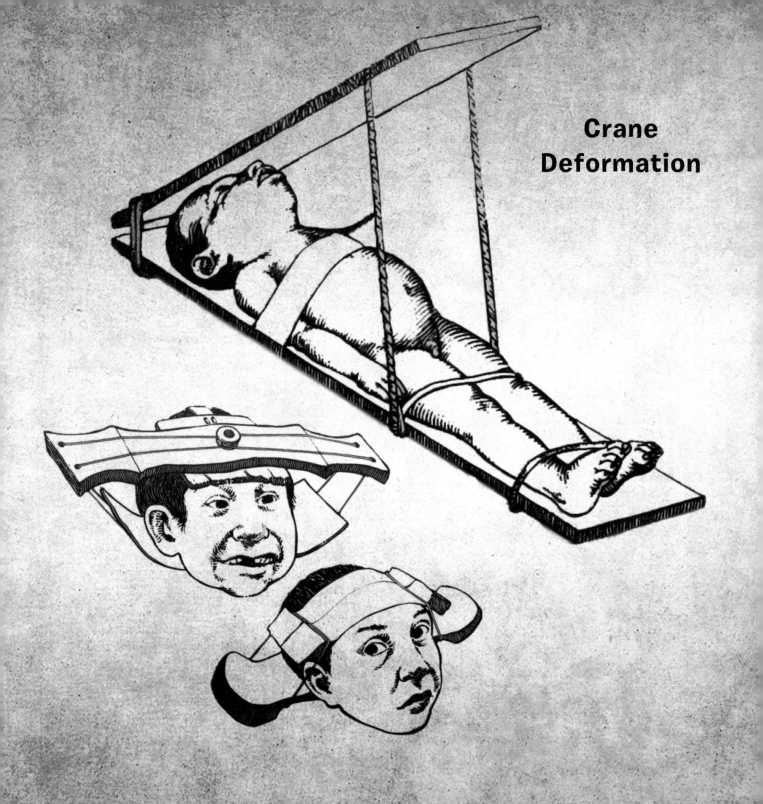

Crane
Deformation

For the Mayans, if you had a flat forehead and crossed eyes, you were especially beautiful! They bound boards to their children's heads to encourage the bones to form in the desired way, and trained the children so their eyes were crossed.

Mayans who wanted to look super beautiful would have cuts made in their skin to form patterns of scars. The nobility would have their teeth filed so the teeth looked like fangs!

The Aztecs, to the north, had a complex religious structure that required regular blood sacrifice to help their gods in a struggle against the forces of chaos.

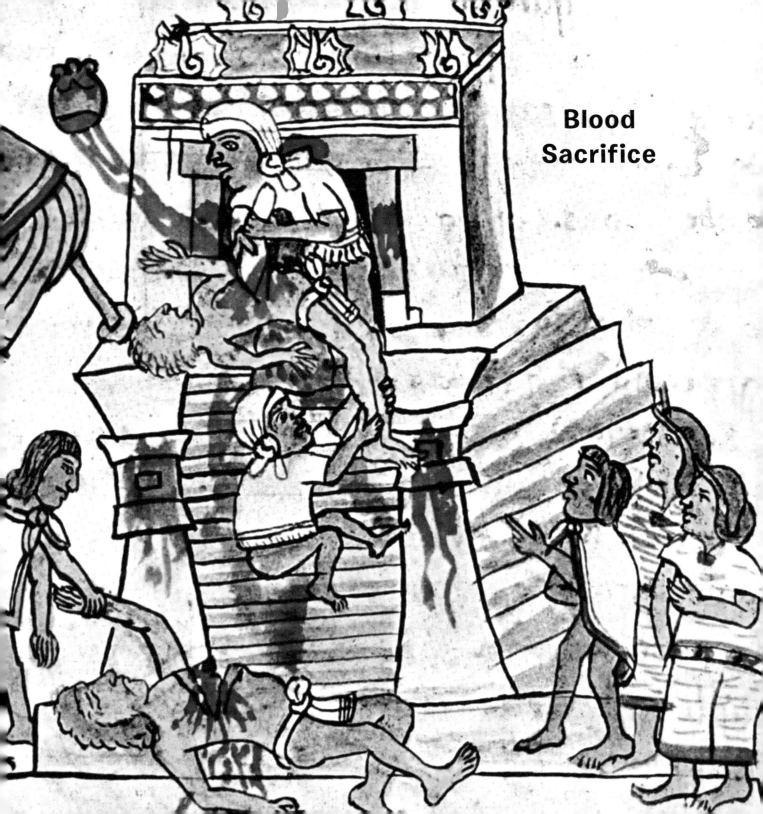

Blood
Sacrifice

The Mayans also made use of blood sacrifice, but their people normally offered some blood, but did not have to sacrifice their lives. However, human sacrifices were needed for some rituals, and this is part of what stimulated the Mayans to conduct wars against other people: they needed to capture brave, strong fighters from other armies who would make worthy offerings to the Mayan gods.

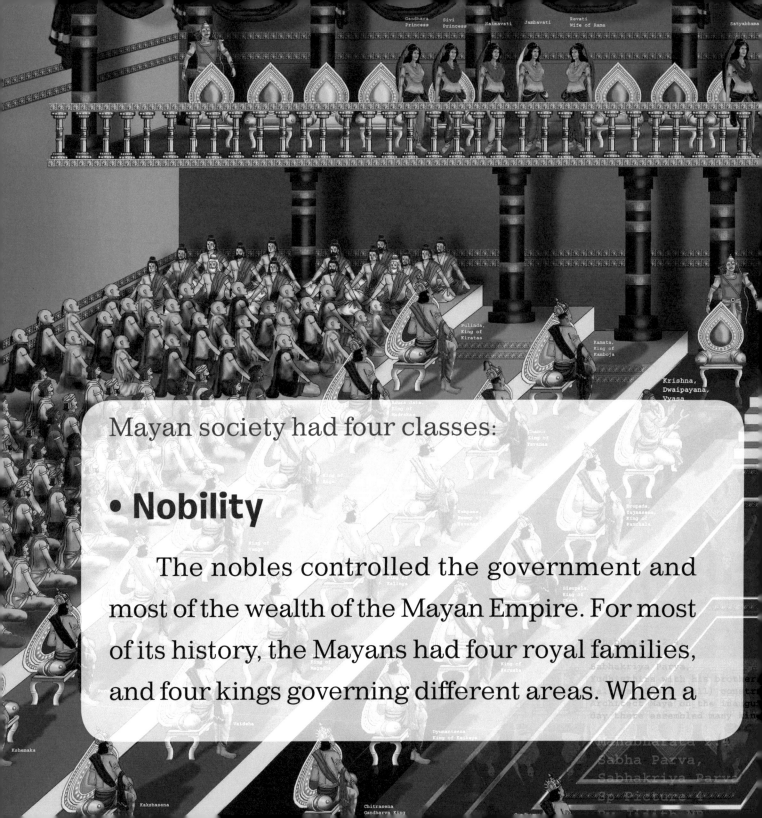

Mayan society had four classes:

• Nobility

The nobles controlled the government and most of the wealth of the Mayan Empire. For most of its history, the Mayans had four royal families, and four kings governing different areas. When a

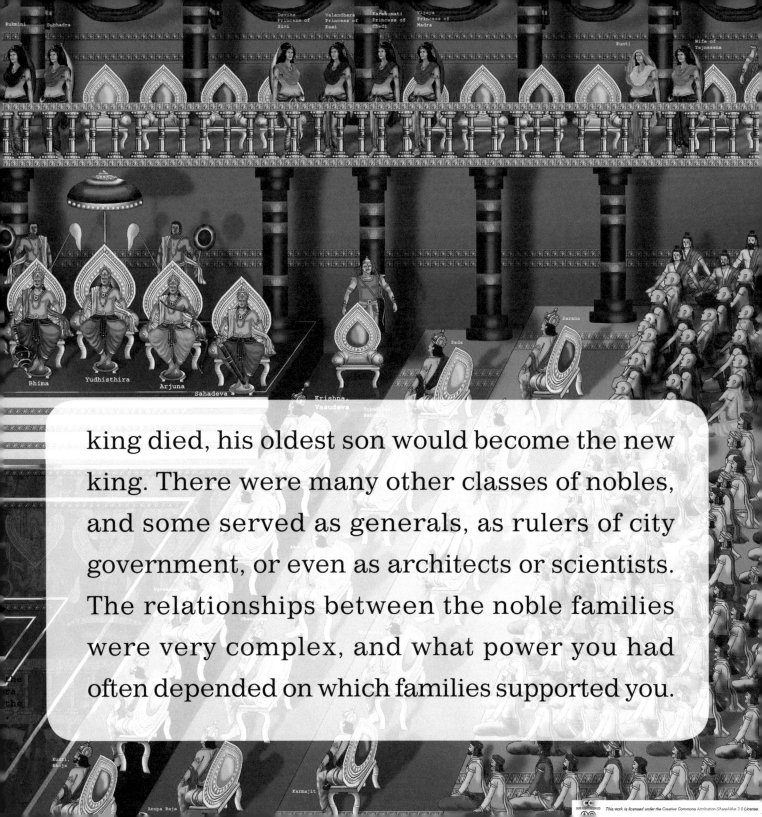

king died, his oldest son would become the new king. There were many other classes of nobles, and some served as generals, as rulers of city government, or even as architects or scientists. The relationships between the noble families were very complex, and what power you had often depended on which families supported you.

• Priests

The kings were also part of the priestly class, but there were a great number of priests and religious servants to manage the complex rituals of the Mayan religion.

• Peasants

Most of the Mayans were of the peasant or commoner class, and most of them were farmers. They would also serve in the army as foot soldiers as needed. From this class came the labor force to build the Mayans' incredible buildings.

• Slaves

At the very bottom of the social heap were slaves. Slaves provided an additional source of physical labor, and often were used in sacrificial ceremonies.

Many slaves had been soldiers captured by the Mayan forces, but you could also become a slave by breaking laws and getting caught.

Mayan Calendar

THE CLASSIC PERIOD

The period from 300 to 900 CE is sometimes called the Classic Period of Mayan culture. During this time the Mayans elaborated their written language, improved their calendar, developed their complex social order, and expanded their borders.

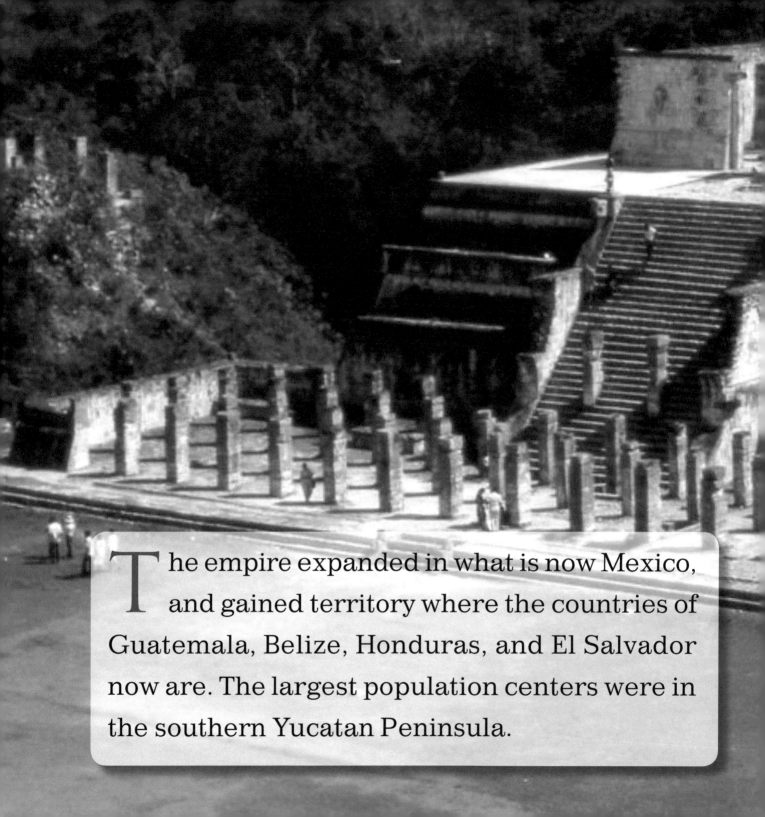

The empire expanded in what is now Mexico, and gained territory where the countries of Guatemala, Belize, Honduras, and El Salvador now are. The largest population centers were in the southern Yucatan Peninsula.

Temple of the Warriors

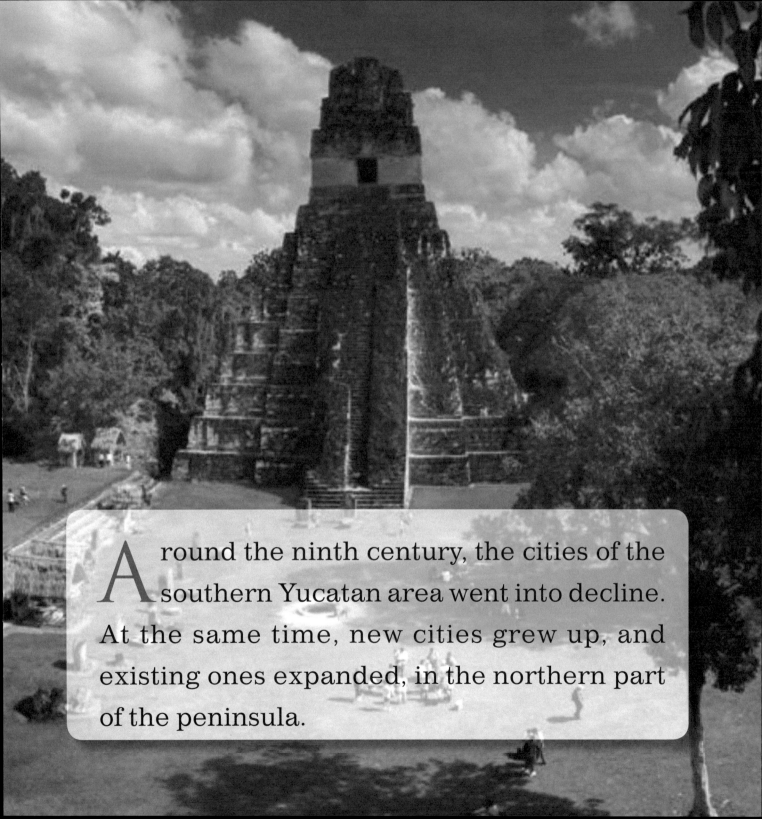

Around the ninth century, the cities of the southern Yucatan area went into decline. At the same time, new cities grew up, and existing ones expanded, in the northern part of the peninsula.

THE LATER PERIOD

The Mayans built remarkable cities between 1000 and 1500 CE, and the ruins of many of these cities are popular tourist destinations today. This was for the most part a time of peace for the Mayans, until a civil war in the middle of the fifteenth century.

Mayan City Ruins

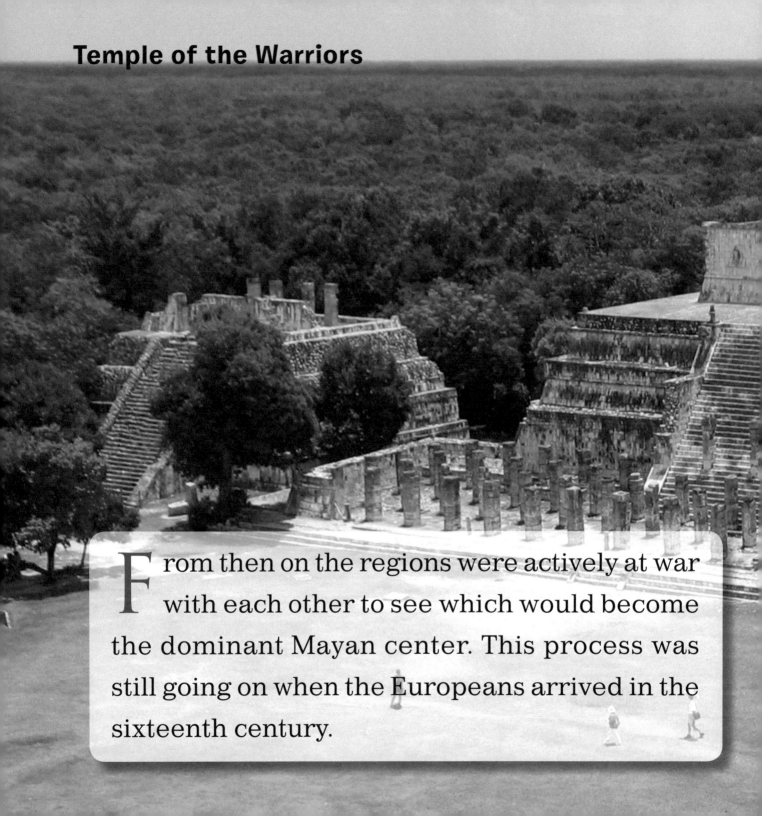

Temple of the Warriors

From then on the regions were actively at war with each other to see which would become the dominant Mayan center. This process was still going on when the Europeans arrived in the sixteenth century.

Many of the Mayans' cities have complicated histories, and we know much less than the full story. Chichen Itza, for instance, started growing as a city sometime after 500 CE. After 900 CE, when it was a large and powerful center, the Mayans abandoned it for some reason we do not know. They moved back into the city about one hundred years later, and not long after that it was attacked and defeated by the Toltec people who lived further north in what is now Mexico. Finally, the Mayans abandoned the city around 1300.

Chichen Itza

COLLISION WITH THE EUROPEANS

Christopher Columbus heard about the peoples of the Yucatan during his voyages to the Caribbean. The first Europeans saw the coast of the peninsula in 1506, and in 1511 a Spanish ship was wrecked on the island of Cozumel. Of the twenty men in the crew, the Mayans sacrificed several to their gods.

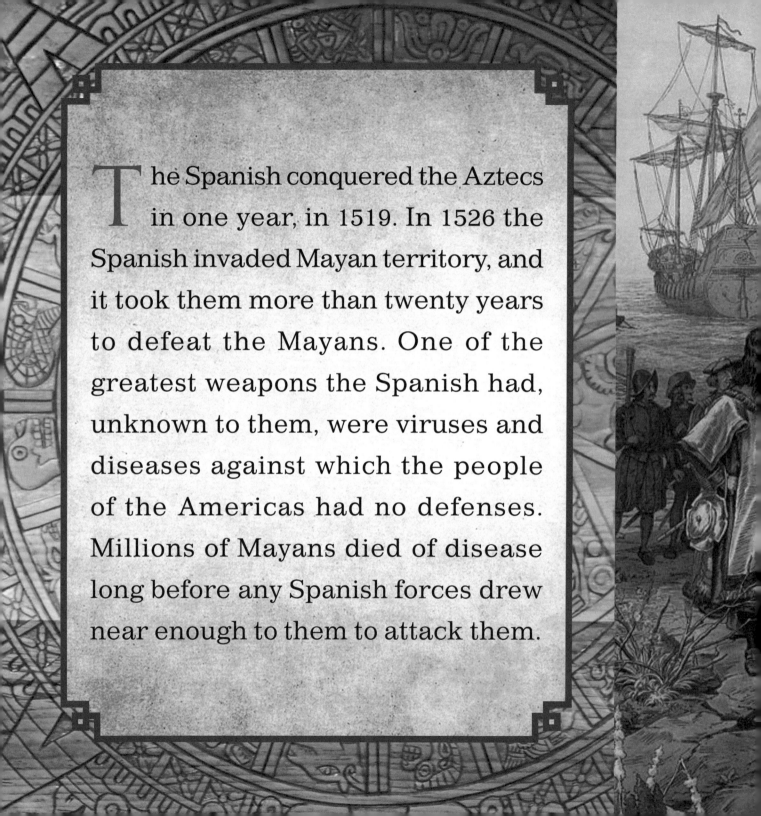

The Spanish conquered the Aztecs in one year, in 1519. In 1526 the Spanish invaded Mayan territory, and it took them more than twenty years to defeat the Mayans. One of the greatest weapons the Spanish had, unknown to them, were viruses and diseases against which the people of the Americas had no defenses. Millions of Mayans died of disease long before any Spanish forces drew near enough to them to attack them.

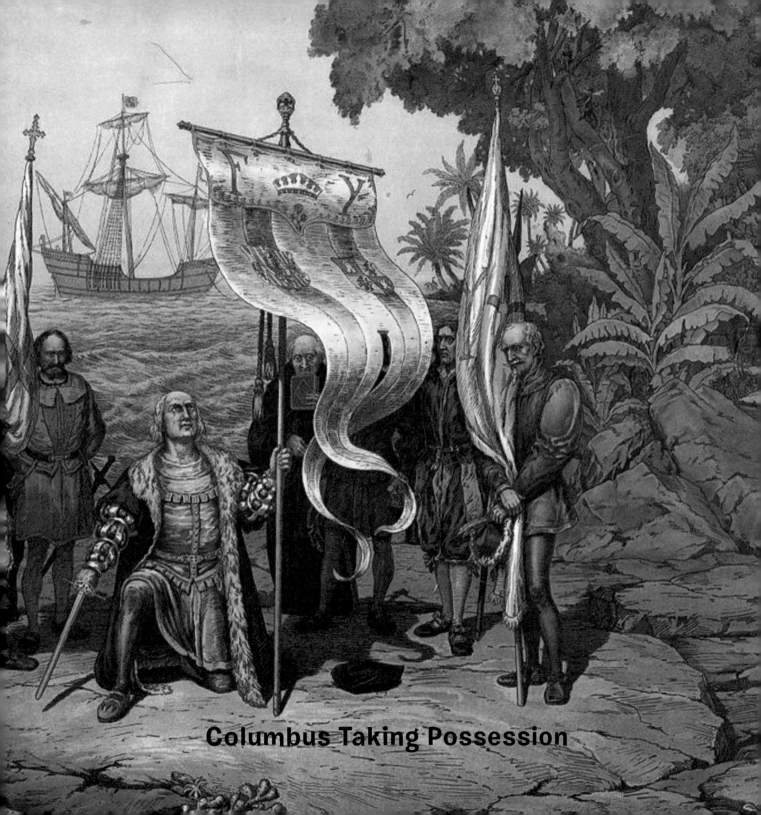

Columbus Taking Possession

Machu Picchu

The Spanish broke up the old system of Mayan government, moved the Mayans into villages, and forced them to pay heavy taxes. The Spanish killed all the Mayan clergy they could find and burned all the religious and historical texts they could get their hands on. This is one reason we know less than we would want to know about Mayan history.

The Mayans continued periodic revolts against the Spanish, and then the Mexican government. In a major struggle for independence in 1846, the Mayans regained almost 90 percent of their traditional territory before they were forced back into their villages. However, they continued to fight, and to hold off the federal army, until 1901.

Even after the government of Mexico had gained control of all Mayan territory, it was largely a closed area to non-Mayans. This only changed during the 1960s as hotels, resorts, and highways started being built along the coast.

Tulum, Mexico, Beach

MAYANS TODAY

The Mayan culture continues today. More than 350,000 people in the Yucatan Peninsula speak Mayan as their first language, and Spanish (the official language of Mexico) as their second language.

PALACE OF FINE ARTS,
MEXICO CITY

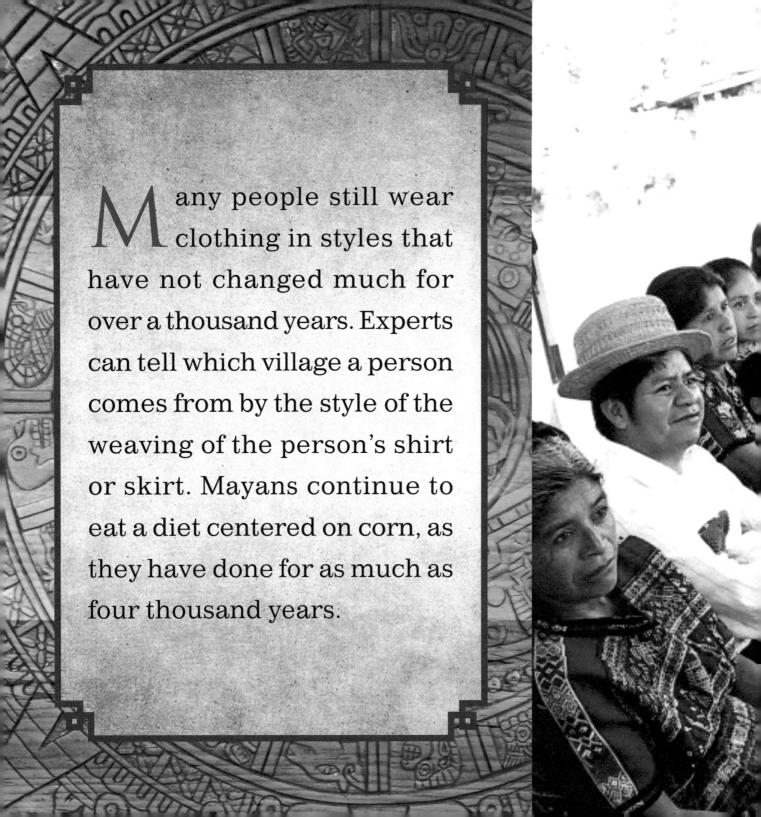

Many people still wear clothing in styles that have not changed much for over a thousand years. Experts can tell which village a person comes from by the style of the weaving of the person's shirt or skirt. Mayans continue to eat a diet centered on corn, as they have done for as much as four thousand years.

Today's Mayans

MORE ABOUT THE MAYANS

The Mayans created a great, complex, and enduring society and culture. Learn more about it in Baby Professor books like The Mayan Cities, The Mayans' Calendars and Advanced Writing Systems, The Mayans Gave Us Their Art and Architecture, and The Daily Life of a Mayan Family